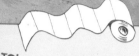

TO:

FROM:

D0122964

To Vicky Stratton: a good friend,
a good mother, a fairly regular ex-wife

Illustrations copyright © 2003 Richard A. Goldberg

Designed by Taryn Sefecka

Copyright © 2004
Peter Pauper Press, Inc.
202 Mamaroneck Avenue
White Plains, NY 10601
All rights reserved
ISBN 0-88088-593-9
Printed in China
7 6 5 4 3 2

Visit us at www.peterpauper.com

CONTENTS

INTRODUCTION

It's not talked about much in polite society, but even the most morally upright, fastidious individuals have to squat and grunt. It's the great equalizer, along with death and taxes. Everyone does it, and everyone has his or her own pet phrase for it. Scientifically, we're talking about defecation: that biological

act of eliminating waste prod-
ucts from our bodies.

But, that's too dry and too
hard. Let's throw a little fiber at
it and see if we can loosen that
up a bit. We're talking about
potty here, my friends. We're
talking about going to the loo,
taking the porcelain cruise,
using the facilities, visiting the
little girls' (or boys') room, pow-
dering our noses, or just plain
going to the bathroom.

In this book we've gathered together a variety of interesting facts, amusing jokes and graffiti, and a little history about the bathroom.

SO, HAVE A SEAT, RELAX, DON'T STRAIN TOO HARD, AND ENJOY THE TRIP!

M. W. D.

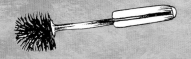

HIGHLIGHTS iN POTTY HISTORY

HERE'S A QUICK VIEW OF POTTYING THROUGH THE AGES:

Archeologists have found evidence of sitting-type toilets in Egypt dating back some 3,000 years.

The Chinese found the oldest working indoor toilet in their country to be 2,000 years old. It belonged to a king of the Western Han Dynasty. The toilet came

complete with running water, a stone seat, and a comfortable armrest.

About the same time as the Chinese, the Romans had a type of indoor toilet that consisted of a hole in the floor above a sluiceway containing running water.

India claims to have

found the oldest indoor toilets, dating back 4,500 years. Each house in the village of Lothal had a toilet with running water connected to a pipe which drained the effluent from the house.

These advances fell out of use, however, and by 500 CE most people simply went wherever the urge struck them. It wasn't uncommon for people to urinate or defecate in the streets in full view of everyone.

YOU SHALL HAVE A DESIGNATED AREA OUTSIDE THE CAMP TO WHICH YOU SHALL GO. WITH YOUR UTENSILS YOU SHALL HAVE A TROWEL; WHEN YOU RELIEVE YOURSELF OUTSIDE, YOU SHALL DIG A HOLE WITH IT AND THEN COVER UP YOUR EXCREMENT.

DEUTERONOMY 23:12-13 NRSV

13

In the home, chamber pots were used to collect wastes, but common practice was to simply throw waste out the window. In England it became customary to warn others by yelling, *Gardez l'eau!* which means, in French, "Watch out for the water!"

The Middle Ages were a foul and messy time for people. In fact, the river Thames caught fire a couple of times due to the overwhelming amount of feces decomposing and producing methane gas.

Finally, in 1596, a hero emerged—the Englishman

Sir John Harington. He invented a flushing toilet, but regrettably his invention was ridiculed and it was gone in a flash, er flush.

Two hundred years later, Alexander Cummings reinvented the flush toilet. This time, the public overflowed with enthusiasm, and

his invention began selling.

In America, two men, James Henry and William Campbell, were granted a patent in 1875 for a "water closet" or flushing toilet. Between 1900 and 1932, the U.S. Patent Office received over 350 applications for new toilet designs.

We owe the basic design of the toilet, as we know it today, to Fred Adee. Early in the 20th century, he solved the overflow problem of his predecessors' models and unveiled the first one-piece, ceramic toilet that worked well, and was odorless.

Today, you can find a

toilet to suit just about everybody's whim. A basic porcelain toilet can be purchased
at the local hardware store for
as little as $30. For those
looking for something fanci-
er, a Japanese company offers
a $2,000 toilet that will
pre-warm the seat for you
and, after you have finished

your business, will squirt warm water onto your backside and then blow dry it!

The ultimate, however, may be the two solid gold toilets that a jeweler had installed in his shop in Hong Kong—part of a gold bathroom valued at $7.6 million.

THE STORY OF
SIR THOMAS CRAPPER

HEREIN LIES THE TALE OF THE TAIL:

If you ask a roomful of people who invented the flush toilet, the odds are that at least one of them will, with authority, offer the name of Sir Thomas Crapper. However, that answer would not be exactly correct. This widely-held belief is based upon a rather specious account of the life of Sir Thomas by Wallace Reyburn. *Flushed with Pride: the Story of Sir Thomas Crapper* tells of how Crapper invented, and was granted a British patent for, the *Silent Valveless Water Waste Preventer.* That device was the forerunner of the flushing mechanism in today's toilets. However, investigative research has shown either that an employee of Crapper actually received that patent, or that Crapper simply bought the rights to the device from its inventor.

Crapper
did exist and was
a well-respected plumbing
manufacturer in England in the
late 19th century. While he did
serve as the royal sanitary engi-
neer for many members of
England's royalty, he was never
knighted.

Thomas Crapper's firm lived

on after his death, and was awarded a contract to construct toilets for the military in World War I. American soldiers were apparently quite amused to use facilities with the name *T. Crapper* printed on the tank. The doughboys began calling the toilets "crappers," and that's how the term came into common usage in America.

Curiously, *crap* as a euphemism existed for at least three

decades before the term *crapper* came into use.

The word *crap*, in all likelihood, is derived from either the Dutch word *krappen,* or the old French *crappe*. In either language, it means "waste, or useless objects." The word *crap* probably came into common usage in America during the great influx of Dutch and German immigrants in the mid-19th century.

GREAT THOUGHTS FROM THE THRONE

HERE WE'VE COLLECTED
SOME GREAT MINDS'
PONDERINGS ABOUT POTTY:

Running is an unnatural act,
except from enemies or
to the bathroom.

AUTHOR UNKNOWN

The Rose Bowl is the only
bowl I've ever seen that
I didn't have to clean.

ERMA BOMBECK

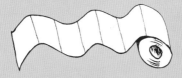

LIFE IS LIKE A ROLL OF
TOILET PAPER. THE CLOSER
IT GETS TO THE END, THE
FASTER IT GOES.

ANDY ROONEY

(ED: WHICH OF US IS

THE MOST OVERRATED ACTIVITY IN HUMANS IS SEXUAL INTERCOURSE, WHILE THE MOST UNDERRATED IS HAVING A BOWEL MOVEMENT.

ANONYMOUS

DOING WHAT WRONG?)

Today you can go to a gas station and find the cash register open and the toilets locked. They must think toilet paper is worth more than money.

JOEY BISHOP

It is difficult to produce a television documentary that is both incisive and probing when every twelve minutes one is interrupted by twelve dancing rabbits singing about toilet paper.

ROD SERLING

EVEN ON THE MOST
EXALTED THRONE IN
THE WORLD WE ARE
ONLY SITTING ON
OUR OWN BOTTOM.

MICHEL DE MONTAIGNE

Excrement can never be
culturally elaborated to the
extent that nutriment can.

MASON COOLEY

WHAT'S ALL THIS I HEAR ABOUT ENDANGERED FECES?

EMILY LATELLA (GILDA RADNER)

Better to have him inside
the tent pissing out,
than outside pissing in.

LYNDON B. JOHNSON,
of J. Edgar Hoover

THERE IS ONLY ONE IMMUTABLE LAW IN LIFE—IN A GENTLEMAN'S TOILET, INCOMING TRAFFIC HAS THE RIGHT OF WAY.

HUGH LEONARD

HOLLYWOOD IS LIKE PICASSO'S BATHROOM.

CANDICE BERGEN

POTTY PARTICULARS

HERE ARE SOME PEE PARTICULARS:

- The kidneys are the body's in-house manufacturers of urine.

- Urine produced by the kidneys enters the bladder through a tube called the ureter.

- The bladder can hold more than two cups of urine!

- Amazingly, the kidneys filter some 425 gallons of blood daily, the waste product of which is pee.

- Eating beets will color your urine red, as will certain food dyes.

Scientists are undecided about asparagus. Only about half the people in the world notice a difference in the smell of their urine after eating asparagus. Some scientists think that's because half of us don't have the gene necessary to break asparagus down to make it smell. Some people think it's because only half of us have the gene necessary to smell it.

IN ROMAN TIMES,
MEN WOULD SEAL
DEALS BY URINATING
TOGETHER AND
"CROSSING THEIR
STREAMS."

©cag2003

HERE ARE SOME DEFECATORY DETAILS:

- One in 100 women potty only once a week.

- If you listen to people, you'd think that most of them go to the toilet every day— but only about 40% of men and 33% of women actually do.

- It takes anywhere from under 20 to over 100 hours for food to make its way through your body before it's ready to be "eliminated."

- The body uses over two gallons of water each day to digest food. Most of the water is reabsorbed back into the bloodstream, however.

- The average weight of a stool (piece of fecal matter) is about 3.5 ounces.

- Stool generally consists of 75% water, retained inside undigested food.

- Poop gets its signature color from bile, a greenish-brown liquid produced in the liver.

BATHROOM HUMOR

HERE ARE SOME OF OUR FAVORITE BATHROOM JOKES:

 drunk man staggered into a Catholic church and sat down in a confession box, saying nothing.

The bewildered priest coughed to attract his attention, but still the man said nothing.

The priest then knocked on the wall three times in a final attempt to get the man to speak.

Finally, the drunk replied, "No use knocking, mate, there's no paper in this one either."

A little old lady goes to the doctor and says, "Doctor, I have this problem with gas, but it really doesn't bother me too much. My farts never smell and are always silent. As a matter of fact, I've farted at least 20 times since I've been here in your office. You didn't know I was farting because they don't smell and are silent."

The doctor says, "I see. Take these pills and come back to see me next week."

The next week the lady comes back. "Doctor," she says, "I don't know what the hell you gave me, but now my farts—although still silent—stink terribly."

The doctor says, "Good! Now that we've cleared up your sinuses, let's work on your hearing."

A drunk gets up from the bar and heads for the bathroom. A few minutes later, a loud, blood-curdling scream is heard coming from that direction.

A few minutes after that, another loud scream echoes through the bar. The bartender goes into the bathroom to investigate what the drunk is screaming about.

The bartender yells, "What's all the screaming about in there? You're scaring my customers!"

The drunk responds, "I'm just sitting here on the toilet and every time I try to flush, something comes up and squeezes the hell out of my testicles."

The bartender opens the door and looks in.

"You idiot! You're sitting on the mop bucket!"

Seventy-year-old George went for his annual physical. All of his tests came back with normal results. Dr. Smith said, "George, everything looks great physically. How are you doing mentally and emotionally? Are you at peace with yourself, and do you have a good relationship with your God?"

George replied, "God and me are tight. He knows I have poor eyesight, so he's fixed it so that when I get up in the middle of the night to go to the bathroom **POOF!** the light goes on when I pee, and then **POOF!** the light goes off when I'm done."

"Wow," commented Dr. Smith, "that's incredible!"

A little later in the day Dr. Smith called George's wife.

"Thelma," he said, "George is just fine. Physically he's great. But, I had to call because I'm in awe of his relationship with God. Is it true that he gets up during the night and **POOF!** the light goes on in the bathroom, and then **POOF!** the light goes off?"

Thelma exclaimed, "That old fool! He's peeing in the refrigerator again!"

A guy showed up at his favorite bar with new eyeglasses. His friends complimented him on how good they looked and he told them how much better he could see because everything looked bigger.

After a few beers, he said. "Gotta go to the toilet; be back in a minute." When he came back, the front of his trousers was all wet.

"What happened to you?" his friends asked.

"I don't know," he replied. "I got in there, pulled it out, and it looked too big to be mine, so I put it back."

A guy walks into a bar and sees his friend, head hanging down, nursing a drink. Naturally he walks over and asks "What's wrong?"

His friend replies, "I'm in deep trouble. This morning the police arrested me for peeing in the shower."

The first guy says, "That's kind of gross but there's no law against it." His friend answers, "I didn't think it was a big deal either but those people at the hardware store are real upset."

A man goes into the restroom, settles in the stall, and tries desperately to relieve himself. After some time, he sighs, and realizes he just can't go.

Suddenly, from the next stall he hears a loud plop.

"Gee, I wish that was me," he says.

A voice on the other side says, "I wish it was you, too. That was my cell phone."

MORE POTTY PARTICULARS

When was toilet paper invented? Some say the Chinese used it in the ninth century BCE. In America, New Yorker Joseph Gayetty is given credit for introducing toilet paper in 1857.

ALMOST
EVERYONE
FEELS BETTER
ABOUT
THEMSELVES
AFTER THEY
FLUSH
THE TOILET.

- The Roman Emperor Vespasian levied a tax on urine when it was used for tanning leather or for cleaning.

- In Rome, at the time of the Emperors, people would make toothpaste, and even mouthwash, from urine.

- Green Bay, Wisconsin, produces more toilet paper than anywhere else in the world.

- More than 70% of people place their toilet paper on the roll with the loose end over the roll.

- In 1913, Scott® Brand Tissue introduced their 1,000 sheet roll at 10 cents per roll, for use as a medical item.

- Based on unofficial research, toilet paper usage varies with education. The more education, the less toilet paper is used.

- An average person uses the toilet 2,500 times a year, or about seven times a day. You spend about three years of your life in the bathroom.

- Females, on average, take three times longer than males to use the bathroom.

- About a third of all Americans flush the toilet while they're still sitting on it.

- Astronauts are not allowed to eat beans before venturing into space.

- Scientists have devised special "space toilets" for use on the international space station. Feces and urine are sucked down separate tubes. Urine is ejected into space. Feces are compressed and stored on board for removal after landing.

Q. WHAT IS THE HOUR OF MAXIMUM TOILET USAGE?

A. IN THE UNITED STATES IT IS HALFTIME OF THE SUPER BOWL.

● According to etymologists, the word *fart* comes from the Old English word *feortan,* presumably of echoic origin, meaning that the word was chosen to sound like the object named.

● A corporate marketing survey studying bathroom habits has found that, when it comes to toilet paper, women are "wadders" and men are "folders."

POTTY HAIKU,

OR "WHAT IS THE SOUND OF ONE HAND FLUSHING?"

HERE ARE
EXAMPLES OF
THIS ANCIENT
FORM OF
EXCREMENTAL
POETRY:

To do number one
or, perhaps do number two—
That is the question.

Water swirls away
Carrying all that's waste.
Damn it! A floater!

In the toilet bowl
of life, strive to be the one
who does the flushing.

For the good of all
we must lift the seat and try
to tinkle neatly.

I am without joy
For I can find no toilet
paper in this stall.

It is far better
To be regular than to
have bowels of pain.

BIRDS FALL FROM
THE TREES.

SMALL ANIMALS
SNEER AT ME.

I HAVE SHAT OUTSIDE.

Again, I must go
Three times in only one hour
It must be the beer.

Watch the water rise
Wish desperately not to
need the plunger.

I must leave, my love,
for if I don't, I will fart
and you will smell it.

GRAFFITI

HERE WE'VE COLLECTED SOME NOT-SO-GREAT MINDS' WRITINGS ON BATHROOM WALLS:

(ON DOOR, BY HANDLE)
John Locke

(ON STALL DOOR)
Patrons are requested to
remain seated throughout
the entire performance.

If you sprinkle while
you tinkle, be a sweetie
and wipe the seatie.

(ABOVE CHURCH URINAL)
The eyes of the Lord
are upon you. Don't miss.

No matter how you squeeze
and dance, the last few drops
go down your pants.

Here I sit, same as ever, took
a dump and pulled the lever.

Urinal Cakes—they're not
just for breakfast anymore!

Here I sit broken-hearted—paid
a quarter and only farted.

KIDS' GRAFFITI:

Beans, beans, the magical fruit
The more you eat, the more you **TOOT!**
The more you **TOOT**, the better you feel,
So eat your beans at every meal!

IS THERE A JOHN
IN YOUR HOUSE? NO?
THEN HOW DO
YOU GO TO THE
BATHROOM?

POTTYSCOPES—
LIKE HOROSCOPES,
ONLY CRAPPIER

WELCOME TO YOUR POTTYSCOPE. HERE YOU WILL FIND THE INFORMATION AND INSIGHTS YOU NEED TO MAKE YOUR BATHROOM EXPERIENCE A MORE ASS-TROLOGICALLY REWARDING EXPERIENCE:

THE GREAT CRAPPINI, POTTYSCOPER TO THE STARS, HAS GAZED INTO HER CRYSTAL BOWL TO CONCOCT THE FOLLOWING FECAL CHARTS:

So, what's your sign?

OCCUPADO?

ARIES

(MARCH 21–APRIL 20)

You have to be the first one in the bathroom in the morning, and, since you're a person of action, you don't spend very much time there, either. When you go, you go. Your commode is first-rate, but utilitarian. In all likelihood it has a quick-to-clean, plastic toilet seat. Your choice of toilet paper is probably something that you grabbed as you were running through the store. As Aries is ever the starter, seldom the finisher, your bathroom is probably in an early, never-to-be-completed state of renovation.

TAURUS

(April 21–May 21)

When you go, you don't come out until the job is finished. However, your throne is extremely comfortable, probably with a padded seat. You'd also prefer it to be "pre-warmed" by someone else. Your toilet paper is the most satiny, gentlest-to-the-bottom variety. You probably have some pre-moistened, perfumed towelettes and a can of bathroom spray available as well. Business-minded Taurus likes to catch up on back issues of *The Wall Street Journal* or *Financial Times*. Best to put that down-time to practical use!

GEMINI

(May 22-June 21)

A Gemini's abdominal constitution can be delicate, so, when you have to go, you have to go. Your choice of a commode is well-researched and well thought out—although you may have thrown all logic aside and just picked one out that you like. You probably change your choice of toilet paper often, after you think it through, and discuss your options with friends, of course. Gemini is the most likely sign of the Zodiac to have a phone in the bathroom. No time to be incommunicado!

CANCER

(JUNE 22–JULY 22)

You have the same kind of toilet that you remember having as a child, right down to the handmade rugs and frilly tissue box holder. Your choice of toilet paper is based on how you're feeling when you buy it. Cancer's bathroom bookcase will be filled with country living and family-oriented reading fare. Be careful with the spicy foods—an upset tummy can put you in a bad mood for days.

LEO

(JULY 23–AUGUST 22)

When a Leo goes, everybody knows about it. You will announce your intentions proudly. Your bathroom is luxurious and first-rate—nothing but the best for you: marble basin, monogrammed towels, the works. No doubt you have the most expensive toilet with a padded, electrically heated seat. Designer toilet paper is a must as well. Why use air freshener? An atomizer of rose oil is much more regal, and befitting Leo's stature. And you keep those movie magazines handy, because they remind you of the star that you are!

VIRGO

(AUGUST 23–SEPTEMBER 22)

You can set your watch by your potty habits, Virgo: same time, every day, guaranteed. You have exactly the right throne for you, no more and no less. The seat is functional and serves its purpose—probably in Spartan white or ultra-chic black, along with dazzling operating-room bright lighting. Virgo's toilet and seat are spotless and sanitized, as is the rest of the bathroom. The economical white paper on the roll had better do the job completely; otherwise, you'll get one that will. Sadly, Virgo is the most likely sign of the Zodiac to be constipated.

LIBRA

(SEPTEMBER 23–OCTOBER 23)

Libra goes to the bathroom only after everyone else has had a chance to go. That's the only fair thing, after all. Your bathroom is the kind that anyone would be proud to use, and you designed it that way, Libra. You're very conscious of social status so you have just the right commode with just the right seat to make that good, lasting impression on people.

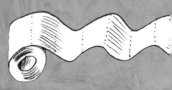

You have everything that anyone could possibly need or use surrounding the throne, as well: lovely rugs, soft scented toilet tissue, expensive air freshener, perhaps even a vase of fresh flowers and a thoughtfully-arranged collection of art and antiques magazines. You have fine taste, Libra, and it shows.

SCORPIO

(October 24–November 22)

Secretive Scorpio, you like to have a bathroom all to yourself. You'd prefer not to answer to anyone when you decorate in sensuous purple or scarlet. Visiting your secret lair is a daily sensual ritual, and you attend to it with great care. When you have to go, you make sure to lock the bathroom door, and clear away all evidence of your presence upon exiting. Your reading fare will be science fiction, or the poetry of Baudelaire—a little light reading!

SAGITTARIUS

(NOVEMBER 23–DECEMBER 21)

Going to the bathroom is an adventure for you, Sagittarius, especially when you commune with the great outdoors on a camping trip (Sagittarius loves to potty outside). Your throne, Sagittarius, is probably the latest and greatest model with the most advanced features. As a matter of fact, you may buy a new seat every few months just because you're tired of looking at the one you have. Sagittarius's bathroom is also well stocked with travel brochures for exotic locales.

CAPRICORN

Going to the bathroom is a serious matter for you, Capricorn, but you'll usually have a witty *bon mot* handy for the occasion. Your choice of potty is practical and inexpensive. You bought the most toilet for the least money. You're especially happy if you can purchase a high-quality model on sale. Capricorn's décor is classical, understated, and never flashy. You always have literary material of the highest caliber handy as well. Why not the classics?